Now I Know

Monkeys

Written by Patricia Whitehead
Illustrated by Bert Dodson

Troll Associates

Library of Congress Cataloging in Publication Data

Whitehead, Patricia.
  Monkeys.

  (Now I know)
  Summary: Simple text and illustrations introduce
the physical characteristics and natural environment
of monkeys and apes.
  1. Monkeys—Juvenile literature. 2. Apes—
Juvenile literature. [1. Monkeys. 2. Apes]
I. Dodson, Bert, ill. II. Title.
QL737.P9W48   599.8'2   81-11439
ISBN 0-89375-670-9   AACR2
ISBN 0-89375-671-7 (pbk.)

10   9   8   7   6   5   4   3   2

Who is that?

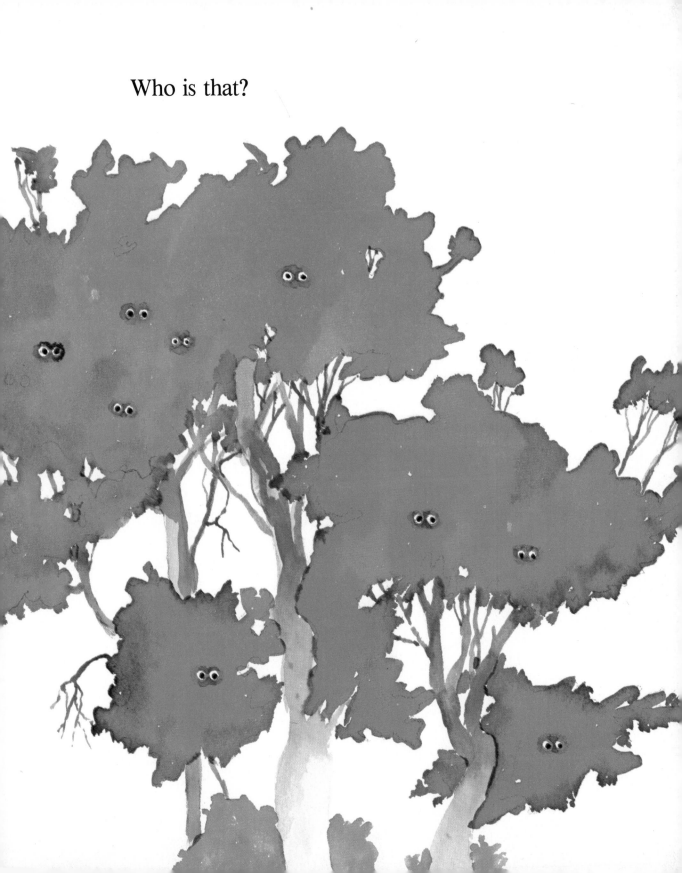

They are in the trees.

Do you know who they are?

They have long arms.

Their eyes are big.

Their feet are like hands.

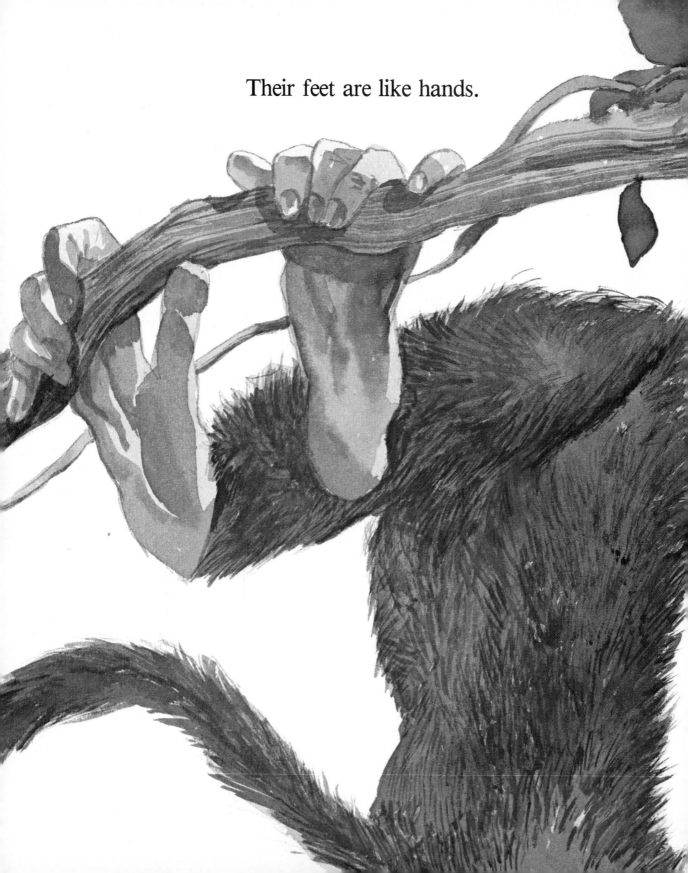

Who are they? Can you guess?

They are the monkeys —

and they are swinging through the trees.

There are all kinds of monkeys.

Some are big. Some are small.

Most monkeys are black, brown, or gray.

But some have spots of red, or
green, or even blue!

This monkey has a big nose.

His nose gets even bigger when he is upset.

Monkeys swing with their hands.

Monkeys swing with their feet.

This little monkey swings with his tail.

He swings with his hands
and his feet and his tail.

Here is a baby monkey. She is going
for a ride on her mother's back.

Up, up, up they go!

This big ape is the monkey's cousin.

Apes are bigger and smarter than monkeys.

A gorilla is an ape.

A gorilla is the biggest ape of all.

Here is a baby gorilla with its mother.

Most monkeys and apes live in forests.

Some live in trees. Some live on the ground.

There are all kinds of monkeys and apes.

But they all have long arms .

And they all love to swing and climb!